ONE PLACE IN TIME

A Special Place in a Splendid Time

Ginger Marshall Martus

Order this book online at www.trafford.com
or email orders@trafford.com

Most Trafford titles are also available at major online book retailers.

Printed in the United States of America.

ISBN: 978-1-4269-7528-8 (sc)
ISBN: 978-1-4269-7529-5 (hc)
ISBN: 978-1-4269-7530-1 (e)

Library of Congress Control Number: 2011915654

Trafford rev. 06/20/2012

 www.trafford.com

North America & international
toll-free: 1 888 232 4444 (USA & Canada)
phone: 250 383 6864 ♦ fax: 812 355 4082

DEDICATED TO

RAYMOND E. MARSHALL

Whose sense of history and encouragement

inspired this writing

ACKNOWLEDGEMENTS...

To those who helped put this together, I want to thank each and every one:

The late Jim Philips, for details about the men and their yachts;

Louie Zwirlein, for updates about the restaurant;

Linda (Marshall) Cashman for secretarial services;

Claire (Marshall) McLean for photos;

Elly Shodell and Staff (of the Port Washington
    Public Library Local History Department) for photos.

...CONTENTS...

INTRODUCTION
Vic Romagna recalls Port Washington where he grew up.

INTRODUCTION

By the Late Vic Romagna

This is a story about growing up on Manhasset Bay; about the places, people and what made it so special for me.

Our family moved to Port Washington in the early 1920s for a number of reasons, such as the direct commuter line into New York City, the school system reported out well, and people with ambition lived here, and of course, the Bay was ideal for sailboat racing along with many other activities.

To keep my brother, Len and I out of Dad's "racing" hair, he bought us a 16 ft. Meteor class sloop which we raced three times a week during the summer months, and we crewed for the older sailors on weekends. The Meteor class was hotly competitive; we had a fine instructor and an astonishing group of talented boat owners. We literally spent all our time in this sport and were avid learners to keep from being disgraced while racing. The amazing Bay offered so much that we took it all in with complacency.

In the pursuit of the game we had to keep our boats in top condition, and we found the best local supplier was Marshall's, where all the gear and equipment was on display, and questions about their use was readily answered by Ray or Monte Marshall or knowledgeable employees who gave us time and valuable information. Marshall's was like a "club" where you could meet and mingle with many yachting personalities which could lead to long questions and answer sessions – a wonderful experience for young fellows like us in a learning curve.

We all remember the Whitney's 74 ft. sleek black APHRODITE as she passed by, leaving the biggest damn swells, so as to knock a small racing boat out of position unless caught perfectly; oh, they would smile and wave to us, but did not recognize our red-faced, fist-clenching signals.

Then the Purdy Boat Company with its group of world-renowned boat builders was part of our life, too. They would build many winning Star boats with unbelievable finishes. In fact, boats from all over came just to be finished by Purdy. Top Star sailor, Adrian Iselin had the ACE, which was kept in the main building where she was constantly being smoothed prior to any race. Many of us crewed for Iselin and learned the infinite skills needed to be at the top of any game. The pursuit of expertise and education was constantly going on around us, and we were absorbing it all like a sponge.

When we left home in the mornings it was with excited anticipation of another adventurous day, and we were on our own. When hungry at lunchtime, we would sometimes catch a flounder, Tommy cod or a crab, build a small fire under some rocks and that was it. Dad was a member of the Port Washington Yacht Club and we could have gone there for a hot dog or sandwich, but would usually hear about it when the monthly bill came in.

Our summers were filled with wondrous things to do and discover, and Port Washington never failed us. We maintained lasting friendships through the years and in all parts of the world, knowing that little can alter the joys of what had been formed in such a wonderful place.

Vic Romagna

ONE PLACE IN TIME

This is the story of the A & R Marshall, Inc. shipyard from the 1920s to 1968 and beyond; how it began and grew into one of the largest and best-known marine service and supply yards on the east coast. It was a time when yards had personalities!

Read about celebrity customers and their yachts, like Bert Lahr, the lion in the "Wizard of Oz," or Ed Wynn in his 80 foot fire-engine red Consolidated, or Leroy Grumman who liked to work on his own 48 foot Chris-Craft, and many others; amusing incidents, near disasters and recollections of a special place in a splendid time, as told by the owner's daughter who called it "my sandbox by the Bay."

Growing up in a shipyard was like growing up with big toys in a sandbox by the Bay. My sandbox was part of a peninsula which juts out into Long Island Sound from the North Shore of Long Island, about 25 miles east of the Big Apple, and with Kings Point, City Island, Rye and Larchmont a stone's throw away.

This once small waterfront town of Port Washington had been known since the middle eighteen-hundreds for the high quality of sand which was mined for many years from both sides of the peninsula. It was a big-buck business in the early days, and strings of four or five barges mounded high with golden sand made their way slowly into New York City to be used in making cement; the saying was, "Cow Bay sand built New York City." Now known as Manhasset Bay, it was once known as Cow Bay because at one time the peninsula was one big cow pasture.

From approximately 1857 until the early nineteen-fifties, about nineteen sand and gravel companies operated at one time or another in this area. Large barrack-type dwellings were built and hundreds of Italian, Polish, Irish, Swedish and Nova Scotian people were imported to labor in the mines. Schools, stores, banks and many commissaries were built to accommodate this growing but isolated population, which became a community unto itself. Some of the early western movies' scenes and action shots were photographed here, using the dug-out pits which produced the high cliffs in the background. Even miners were used as "extras" on location. Yes, fortunes were made from this golden sand.

About the time I started making sand castles, the Bay was alive with all types of boats; houseboats were very much in vogue and many people who had homes in New York City would come out and stay all summer aboard their boats, or rent cottages. The automobile was an established necessity, and wealthy young men were trying out new, innovative seaplanes and speedboats on the Bay.

This was the time of fast commuters, where Gold Cup speedboat races, auto races, fabulous parties at the Sands Point Casino, and seaplane races were held, and where great polo players played; where even the Duke of Windsor played only a few miles away at Westbury. This truly was THE place of the Gatsby era. It was also a time when young fellows with speedboats were quietly recruited with the lure of fast money if they would go out from a secret location along the shore to rendezvous with an innocuous-looking vessel and bring back a load of prohibited booze as fast as possible. They were promised cash, but some never made it back to shore, as they were either hijacked, murdered or drowned.

Along the waterfront were a few stores, workshops, four or five shipyards (at the Ike Smith shipyard, the birth of the Star One Design boat took place in 1911), small docks, one or two good restaurants, plus a number of gin mills; a ferry landing, and the huge Pan American hangers (where aviation history was made).

Four yacht clubs were also located there, all now over one hundred years old: North Shore Yacht Club (founded 1871), Knickerbocker Yacht Club (founded 1874, and sadly now decommissioned), Manhasset Bay Yacht Club (founded 1891) and the Port Washington Yacht Club (founded 1905).

Our family business, known as A & R Marshall, Inc., was one of the early shipyards, and located at 403 Main Street, in Port Washington, NY. It began operation just prior to the depression, in 1928; that was the hard part.

I've been asked many times what the "A" stands for in the title, to which I reply, the "A" stands for Albert, my grandfather (1868-1948) who came to the United States by the "back door," by working his way over from London on a freighter and "jumping ship" at Bayonne, New Jersey in 1888, when he was 20 years old, with little money but lots of talent. This was Grandpa, who was always called "Boss" — with respect! The "R" is for my father, Raymond (1898-1978), who was later joined by his younger brother Montague (1903-1985) known as Monte, and their sister, Dorothy (1899-1972) who was bookkeeper for many years until she married one of the prominent customers in 1937; then Monte's wife Edna (1907-1976) took over as bookkeeper.

It was during these years that many of the rich and famous became good long-time customers and many others also added to the personality of this shipyard. In those days, it was said that each yard had its own personality and reputation, and was a place you identified with.

What "The Boss," Ray and Monte purchased in 1928 was an old building that had been a barn converted into a hotel of rumored reputation. There was a small dock which was enlarged; a crane was purchased, and a large storage shed built later. The inside was remodeled and the marine hardware was increased. Monte built a large workboat which became a familiar sight on the Bay for many years, and was on call 24 hours for emergencies, from downed aircraft to sunken boats.

Ray and Monte had opposite personalities, but seemed to work well together; although Ray, being older, usually had the last say in business matters and held the majority of shares in Marshall Holdings. Ray was a good business man, fair minded, orderly and jovial; whereas Monte was more of the "Popeye the Sailor" type. His gravel voice did not mince words; he spoke like the "salt" he was; was wiry, active, and appeared on the gruff side unless you knew how to butter him up. He would be impatient in dealing with people but was respected, as he was the one who got things done and done right. At about the age of 18 he designed and built a 20 foot speedboat; one of many more he was to build over the years. His powerboat, the 27 foot ARK, was built and launched in 1954; by the way, he called many other boats by the same name. A superb craftsman, he could and did build almost anything from a life-sized figure of his pet dog "Peppy," to seven carved busts of his family.

The "Boss" worked in various capacities in the yard; he could work with iron as well as with wood with great creativity. One time he was working with mahogany and developed wood poisoning, and his whole body turned a dark brown; I'll never forget what a sight he was! All he needed was a coat of varnish and he would be a live, walking figurehead! He could turn a lathe with such precision that the threads of screws or fittings would mesh perfectly; workmen and customers alike would watch and marvel at his workmanship. You could also see the "Boss" on a sunny windless day doing the gold-leaf lettering on boat transoms.

Being primarily a service and repair yard, all types, shapes and sizes of boats and people came and went through the yard; there was a local saying, "others built 'em, Marshall's fixed 'em."

Spring at any shipyard is the most hectic time of year, when people were three deep at the front counter and everyone wanted their boat launched first. At times it looked like the floor of the NYSE – and that's when I would help out.

Ray and Monte had devised a system where boat configurations were cut out in cardboard (laundry shirt boards were used), showing length, width and name of each boat to be stored inside or out. The yard held over 100 boats, and it was quite a sight to see them being moved into launching position, when the skids were greased, and then slowly and gently the boats were pulled and pushed onto the ways for launch. This could only be done at high tide, so it was a frantic few hours to get as many "over" as possible.

Of course, one of the biggest problems was getting the pumps going as soon as they hit the water, and the yard crew knew which ones were the "leakers," so large hand pumps were quickly used at first; it usually took overnight for the boat to swell enough to stay afloat. On one occasion, a new 30 foot powerboat was launched and the pumps hooked up electrically for overnight, and when Monte arrived early the next morning, (you guessed it), she was 75 percent underwater. It seems the electric plug came loose, and there she went. The owner, the late Leo Cardillo, a good-natured fellow, took it in stride much to Monte's chagrin. Leo, who had been a Commodore of the Port Washington Yacht Club, recalled this when he saw me, and laughed!

After each launching, if the owners were present, they would usually offer a round of drinks to the yard crew, so you can imagine at the end of the day everyone went home quite happy.

The yard crew consisted of about 15 to 20 men during the spring and summer months, and it was considered the "in" place to work for high school fellows during the summer, and many a romance bloomed in this sandbox with the girls who were working on their sailboats. The regular staff, which were kept on all winter, had been with the company almost since the beginning: top mechanic Jim who worked over 40 years; Bert Cochran, 35 years; Harry Aarsheim, the Norwegian carpenter and master craftsman, 40 years; and Scotty, 35 years, was also an excellent worker. Pat Patterson was the store manager and Al Carbonell worked in the store with him. Pat and Dad would never miss the New York Boat Show.

The night watchman, Alexander Alexander, known as Sandy was with the company for 39 years, and could sometimes be seen in late afternoon with his dog Jake on the end of a rope. Sandy had such a thick Scottish accent that it was difficult to understand him at times, but he kept his appointed rounds until the day he died.

His living quarters were just off one of the office rooms on the first floor of the old building, and sometimes when the door was open we would dash through holding our noses, as it always had the most God-awful smell coming from his large cooking pot. People would bring him all their extra fish from the day's catch and he would toss them in with a few potatoes, a carrot or two, and that was dinner for the next few days. Even low tide smelled better; no wonder there were always a dozen cats at his back door.

The old original building was demolished between 1947 and 1948, and the large colonial structure (which can be seen today) was erected at 403 Main Street. The stock was increased again, and everything was carried, from Chrysler Crown engines to His Lordship jewelry. In those days, young men from neighboring towns would bicycle all the way over to spend hours looking at the array of merchandise, and dream about the day when they could actually use this good stuff on a boat of their own. There was a 248-page catalog, and orders from around the world were filled.

About 1922, Ray joined the Port Washington Yacht Club (founded in 1905), and later elected Membership Chairman, which office he retained for fifteen years, 1930 to 1945. In the early days, yacht clubs in the area were all looking for new members; as then during the depression years followed by World War II, many clubs were in dire condition with some closing and others holding on precariously.

Because of his position with the Club and his business, new customers and people moving into this community found him most helpful in getting into a yacht club, and the Port Washington

Yacht Club did exceedingly well under his sponsorship. He held this position longer than any other member, and the Club did prosper.

I remember that on a warm, busy spring day a hush suddenly came over the whole yard, when word ricocheted that Frank P. Huckins died unexpectedly; there was silence for a few moments on that May 30, 1951. Later I realized what a revered man he was to all yachtsmen.

During the summer months, when the boats were out of the big shed, it was rented to Philip and Ruth Hunter, who operated a summer theater for about nine years. Known as the Towndock Theater, it was a favorite waterfront attraction. Ruth, a stage veteran, had had the lead as Ellie May in the long-running "Tobacco Road," and had written two books. Philip hosted a radio show. He was an impeccable, dashing, handsomely-dressed man, always with umbrella and derby hat, whereas Ruth was in constant disarray and would sometimes even wear her dress inside-out, looking more like a "bag lady." People thought Philip was a butler and Ruth a chambermaid from one of the big estates in Sands Point as they went about their appointed rounds in town.

This area was a Mecca of the who's who in the yachting world in those days; when you could see Morris and Stanley Rosenfeld in FOTO out in the Sound following the yacht races. It was always a treat when Ed Wynn would stop by to tank up with Texaco in his 80 foot fire-engine red Consolidated yacht, THE CHIEF. Texaco sponsored his New York vaudeville show, "Hells-a-Poppin," while he lived in Great Neck, near Groucho Marx. Then there was Bert Lahr, who played the Lion in the "Wizard of Oz," who owned a small powerboat which he liked to work on. Even without make-up, he looked the part, and sometimes would belly out a roar with his famous sneer if a pretty girl passed by, or if something displeased him.

Leroy Grumman, who was a delightful man, would enjoy working on his own 48 foot Chris Craft, SLIPSTREAM; he would frequently assist top mechanic Jim Philips who was working on the boat at the same time. Both being mechanically-minded, the two got along very well.

It was known that Jim could tell, just from the sound of a boat's engine coming or going from the Bay, and from a long distance off, whose boat it was, without even seeing it. He had worked on and knew so many engines that he probably could have written a book about them. Jim also contributed his vast knowledge about the boats and people.

One day, a very large yacht tied up at the dock, and out stepped a few men dressed in flowing Arab robes. Also with them was a young man about 15 years old. Monte was on the scene to give gas, and assumed one of the older men was the Captain or at least in charge; as it turned out, it seems they all consulted the young lad before any decisions were made. After some friendly conversation, Monte found out the young fellow was actually a Prince or a young King of one of the Middle-East nations, who was on holiday while attending school in this country. So, you never knew who was going to pull up to the dock.

Then there were the stories about Prince Michael Romanoff, the great imposter, who claimed to be a direct descendant of the Royal Imperial Russian Romanoffs, but no one knew for sure. There were many whispers about this ugly but elegant man with a regal bearing and proper manners. One of the rumors was that he owned a houseboat in the Bay, and that a procurer was supplying prostitutes to an occupant that lived aboard who was in a constant stupor, but it seems the crew were the ones that were really enjoying the visits, and one of the crew, a Danish fellow, married one of the visitors. He was known as "The Great Dane."

One day, when the "Prince" and his entourage stopped by for gas, he came up the gangway where Mother and I were standing, and as a little girl being introduced to a prince (Mother was very impressed and told me to be nice), I made the unpardonable comment, "I don't like that man."

There were many amusing and also dangerous incidents over the years, such as the time Monte was about to lock up the big shed doors at closing time, and as always would call out, "anyone still inside"? One evening, he heard a faint call for help, and upon investigation found a customer on his knees with his right hand extended up toward the bottom of his boat, with one finger protruding into a newly-drilled small hole. Seems he drilled the hole, then stuck his finger in to clean out the sawdust, when he couldn't get it out again; with a bit of assistance he was freed from an embarrassing overnight stay in a cramped position.

There was also the time when the 1938 hurricane blew in on September 21st, and put the businesses along the waterfront under water up to the main road. Buried in the driveway between the big shed and the store were large gasoline tanks that serviced the three pumps in front of the store. As darkness settled in that evening, while doing what they could to secure the floating debris, Monte noticed a film of rainbow colors floating on top of the water in the driveway, which meant that gasoline was leaking from the underground tanks. At the Horseshoe, a gin mill next door operated by two old maids, the McGrath sisters and their golden cocker spaniel, a small gathering of local waterfront people were having their usual evening snorts by candlelight and of course smoking, in spite of the water seeping in around them. Whereupon Monte flung open the door and quickly pointed out in his salty tongue that if they valued their hides and businesses, they'd better damn well put out the candles and cigarettes NOW, as the whole waterfront could ignite at any moment! Needless to say, flashlights were quickly grabbed, and Monte was credited with preventing a disaster.

Another time, Ray was using the family boat ALDO, a 40 foot Balzer-Jonesport, to tow some young sailors in Blue Jays over to Larchmont Yacht Club so they could participate in Larchmont Race Week. It was an overcast, sultry July day, and just before arriving at Larchmont, a bolt of lightning struck the military mast and smoke began to pour from the cabin below. After the initial stunning shock, which was more like an explosion, he quickly shut the motor off and got the fire extinguisher, and looked below expecting the worst. In the meantime, the sailors, who actually saw the lightning strike, cast off immediately, and probably all turned white; they were later picked up and towed in. The boat was not on fire, but the cabin was in disarray from the jolt. The ship-to-shore radio had jumped off its position; the *Daily News* looked like it had been through a shredder; even the leads in the pencils were forced out. Many items that had been secure had all come loose from their spots. Anyone who has been that close to lightning knows what this is like. The glass hinged vents on the outside cabin deck were all cracked and smoked, but not broken. No one was injured in this frightful incident.

In all the years of operation, there was never a serious fire, the dread of any shipyard. Other yards had fires; in 1914 Manhasset Bay Shipbuilding & Repair Co., a shipyard located adjacent to the Port Washington Yacht Club, was destroyed by fire and many boats were lost. Then in 1974, a tragic fire erupted at the then Petersen Shipyard, next to the Manhasset Bay Yacht Club, where a fleet of 15, 27 foot mahogany Resolutes were kept. Monte said the one thing he insisted on was a clean yard, which he felt was the reason for no fires; this is where "neatness REALLY counts."

Resolutes were designed by William H. Tripp, they were built and shipped over from Norway under the "fathership" of James B. Moore.

While in high school, I would occasionally have an evening party aboard the ALDO. Dad would take us over to Rye Beach for fun and games; other times we would anchor right off the runway at LaGuardia Airport. This was always a thrill, as the planes' landing lights would light up the cabin roof while we all stood up and waved to the pilot; you felt you could almost touch the wheels. . . I wonder what the pilots thought about all of this. Remember, this was in the BJ era, Before Jets.

Now, some words about the neighbors. On the right side of the 403 Main Street Building is the well-known, if not famous, Louie's Shore Restaurant, then operated by the fourth generation of the Zwirlein family. Gordon and Louis, sons of father Louis Sr., ran the business for many years. Louis Jr., known to many as Dick, and I went through the local schools together and have always been friends.

Dick and his wife, Diane, retired in 1988 and moved to Florida. Diana passed away in 1998 and Dick remarried in 2002. Gordon, the eldest of the two brothers and his late wife Georgette, with their two sons Jay and Randy, then operated the business. Gordon passed away in about 2003 and Georgette died in 2006. Jay moved to Crisfield, Maryland and Randy, who had cancer, died about 2001. Louie's Restaurant was sold to Martin Picone in 2002 but kept the famous name. Martin renovated extensively and it is still a favorite place.

Earlier, at 4:30 P.M. each day, Ray and Monte would go over to Louie's for their afternoon drink, going back to the store at 6:00 P.M. for closing. As Louis Zwirlein remembers, on Saturday a lot of the regulars would gather. It was like a reunion and the bartender of over 20 years, Chuck, remembers them well.

An amusing incident took place many summers ago when the actor Rex Harrison (*My Fair Lady*), and his wife Kay Kendall, were summering at the John H. Whitney boathouse in nearby Plandome. This unique boathouse built in 1929, has large sliding doors to accommodate seaplanes and boats, with a ramp leading to the water's edge. One day, Harrison parked his car in the narrow alley between the restaurant and the Marshall store where he was shopping. With the store full of people, a loud bellowing voice said, "who is parked in MY driveway"? Gordon had bounded in, ready to chew out the guilty party, but when the tall, dignified Rex Harrison acknowledged that it was his car, Gordon became almost apologetic, and even invited him over to the restaurant for a drink.

Directly to the left of the big shed at 405 Main Street was a small restaurant known at one time as the "Blue Bell," owned by the Bellas family. It was enlarged over the years, and became a favorite waterfront eatery called "Jimmy's Backyard," operated by Mr. Bellas Sr. and son Jimmy. Jimmy's Backyard was sold in the sixties. The restaurant re-opened on upper Main Street, and the building changed hands and names several times.

Immediately next door to that was the more-than 100-year-old Knickerbocker Yacht Club, founded in 1874. This Club holds fond memories for me, as a child in the 1930s; when "The Boss" and Ray were running the shipyard, "The Boss" became a member of the Club, and we frequently had lunch there. This is where winter Frostbite sailing originated on a cold New Years' Day in 1931; still an annual event, it is now hosted by their immediate neighbor, the 100-year-old Manhasset Bay Yacht Club (founded 1891).

During the early part of World War II, the Navy sent out scouts to search the shipyards along the coasts to commandeer private and commercial vessels that could be pressed into the War effort. Once the scouts selected a boat, no one was allowed to board the craft henceforth, not even the owner. It was, at that moment, declared government property. The deal was this: the Navy or Coast Guard would use the vessel as long as needed, and then return it, if possible, as is. Of course, most owners were more than happy to assist in this dire time. During the War, the identification numbers on all vessels were 10" numerals on both sides of the bow.

The yacht I'm most familiar with was the 50 foot motorsailer, ESCAPE, owned by Fred H. Walsh, which was built and launched in July, 1939 from the Marshall yard. The Navy took possession of her in 1942 and returned her three years later; having been painted completely gray, she earned six Chevrons, one for each six months' of service. When returned to the yard, Monte said, "it took just about as long to restore her as it did to build her." The most visible signs of wear that I noticed were to the stair treads to the below cabin, which were almost worn through. Many men who served aboard these vessels have interesting stories to tell.

An amusing incident centers on the early pioneer flights of the Pan American flying boats, or "Clippers" as they were called. Their main area of operation was from huge hangers located on Manhasset Isle's waterfront, near where they landed and from which they departed for Bermuda, the Azores or England in the early 1930s. They had one big obstacle on the Bay, which was the 16 foot Meteor one-design sailboat that was the most popular racing boat at that time. Designed by Charles D. Mower in 1927, 46 were built and actively raced into the 1960s. The story goes, as told by Vic Romagna (a local top sailor who went on to be spinnaker man on Weatherly in the 1962 America's Cup races and later instructor at the Naval Academy at Annapolis), that the fleet of Meteors always sailed on a course that was in the direct line of a landing "Clipper," which was a potential disaster. Picture a bowling ball heading for a strike! The sailors, being typical teenagers, knew that sailboats had the "right of way," much to the consternation of the pilots, who sometimes had to circle once or twice before landing. This went on for a while until the Pan Am people had enough of this arrogance, and decided to hold a "pow-wow" at one of the yacht clubs, to try to impress the young sailors the seriousness of this problem. They offered to take a group up for a flight in a "flying boat" and show them first-hand the problem of trying to land a big plane with a fleet of little sailboats in the landing path. . . well, that did it! The sailors were thrilled with the ride, and finally admitted the pilots really did have a problem, and assured them they would alter their course.

There was a rash of tragic club fires in the 1950s that not only destroyed lovely old buildings, but a heritage of historical material and trophies all went up in smoke. The fires of note in the immediate area were, the American Yacht Club, founded in 1883 at Rye, New York, burned to the ground on July 27, 1951. Then the Plandome Country Club went up in flames on December 24, 1957, and on August 15, 1980, the Sea Cliff Yacht Club burned; rebuilt, it celebrated its 100th anniversary in 1992.

The 1905 Port Washington Yacht Club caught fire on the night of January 30, 1954. Monte and his wife, Edna, were at the Club that evening, and later commented that it seemed overheated. The furnace was located under the ladies' lounge, alongside a wide staircase. It had been previously speculated that if a fire ever occurred, people would have been trapped, with only one other small exit located on the second floor veranda, which was the dining room. The cause was suspected to be electrical, and as sad members gathered the following morning to view the ruins, only the chimney was standing. By late afternoon, a rendering of the new clubhouse was posted, which lifted spirits, and by the following spring a cinderblock structure was erected. Not exactly aesthetically attractive to many, it has since mellowed and is homeport to many sailors in the area. Today, there are very few members who remember the "old club;" I am one of those few.

Another fire of note destroyed a famous old landmark located on Plum Point at the tip of Sands Point. This site was known by various names, such as the Sands Point Casino and lastly, the Sands Point

Beach and Racquet Club. It was destroyed on March 19, 1986. At one time, the Club was a well-known, glamorous spot for entertaining: Tommy Dorsey, Glenn Miller and others played there. It was frequented by famous, infamous and even notorious celebrities; even F. Scott Fitzgerald was known to have spent many "madly exhilarating nights" there. One highly publicized event took place in August, 1933, when Senator Huey Long, former Governor of Louisiana was one of the most controversial politicians of his time, known for his outrageous behavior usually brought on by overindulgence in "spirits." While visiting friends in Sands Point, and after a few drinks at the hosts' home, the group headed over to the Sands Point Club. The incident occurred later in the men's room, and when Long returned to the table with a bloody eye, Long requested that they leave. When asked what happened, Long insisted that he was attacked by a group of gangsters. It made the headlines, but no one knew for sure what actually took place. Huey Long was assassinated in 1935.

As mentioned earlier, the Star one-design boat originated in the office of William Gardner, a well-known naval architect, and the boat was designed about 1911. George A. Corey, Commodore of the Manhasset Bay Yacht Club was known as the "Father of the Stars," and George W. Elder, Commodore of the Port Washington Yacht Club were both good friends, and promoted this new innovative sailboat for many years. A local boatyard, owned by Isaac Smith, built the first 22 Stars at $265 each. For the next 14 years, it gained rapid popularity and is still raced competitively today. The first National Regatta was held in 1922; six boats raced, with the winner as William Inslee. This first race was hosted by the Bayside, Manhasset and Port Washington Yacht Clubs. In 1923, 8 boats raced in the

First International Regatta with the winner, again, William Inslee. In 1924 there were 10 boats, and the winner was John Robinson; and the 1925 race saw 15 boats and the winner was Adrian Iselin II of the Port Washington Yacht Club. The A & R Marshall shipyard was given the job of hauling the boats out each day and putting them over again the following morning for the five-day regatta.

And so, after forty years of active business, Ray and Monte could foresee the coming of fiberglass in the early 1950s. They commented that it would mean the eventual demise of the skilled crafts that were so important to wooden boats; the long-time employees could smell that new "stinky stuff" in the wind, and they knew a change would be coming to the yard in the near future.

It was a difficult decision, as they had devoted their lives to the business; even with Pat Patterson as Manager, it was becoming more complex and difficult to operate, and with no heir interested in carrying on, the only solution they could see was to sell the business. Monte had one son, Robert, an engineering graduate of Cornell University who had worked with Monte for a few years, but felt his talents lay in another direction. He was with an engineering firm for many years. He lives in Connecticut and has three children and nine grandchildren. Ray had seven children. Two children were with his first wife, Dorothy Fenn, me and my sister Claire. I lived for 40 years in New Jersey with my late husband, Joe, and now live in Easton, Maryland. Claire raised show dogs (Bouvier des Flanders and Portuguese Water Dogs) on the western shore of the Chesapeake Bay and now lives in Annapolis, Maryland. She and her husband Charles (now divorced), a retired Lt. Colonel, have four grown children and nine grandchildren. The five other children were with his second wife, Edith Townshend, and four are now located in the west: Bill is in South Dakota with his wife, Joyce and has three sons and one grandchild; Mary Elizabeth (Liz) is in Washington State, Chris in Colorado, and Charles in Nevada. Linda and her husband Dick still lives on Long Island, and has one child and two grandchildren.

And so ended an era in the local maritime annals of Port Washington, a special place in a splendid time.

At the left is Ray Marshall and at the right is Monte, having just
returned from having lunch at Louie's

Exterior of the early shipyard at 403 Main Street, Port Washington. This building was at one time the Bayview Hotel. It was torn down in 1947 to make way for new construction.

This is the new building after construction. Monte Marshall made the signs and the half models of sailboats at the entrance.

Left is Monte Marshall in front of the A&R Marshall shipyard during construction of the new building.

Aerial view of shipyard shows boats stored for Winter. Notice the large GULF barge in front of the dock.

This is the building next door to 405 Main Street where boats were stored under cover during winter months and where the Towndock Theater was held in summer months.

Raymond E. Marshall poses for a DuPont nylon rope ad at the Shipyard.

PROMINENT CUSTOMERS AND OTHER PERSONALITIES

Carl G. Fisher: Early real estate developer of Miami, Montauk Point and Bayview Colony, a group of custom homes on the waterfront in Port Washington, where his home is still occupied. He set up the Purdy Boat Co. Inc. about 1925

Caleb S. Bragg: A wealthy sportsman and industrialist who owned fast cars, airplanes and boats. Owner of the famous BABY BOOTLEGGER, winner of Gold Cup races, plus YO HO HO II, a 50 foot power boat designed by Purdy in 1929.

Jay Holmes: Holmes married one of the Fleischmann daughters, and lived in an English Gothic mansion in Sands Point. He owned a 93 foot powerboat designed by George F. Crouch, built by Harry Nevins at City Island in 1937, named SEMLOH.

Harold S. Vanderbilt: His 150 foot Purdy-designed powerboat, VARA, was built by Herreshoff in 1928 and registered in Port Washington.

John J. Warsaw:	Beloved Commodore of the Knickerbocker Yacht Club, he had a splendid high-powered commuter, the 60 foot SPEEDALONG, built by Consolidated Shipyard in 1928 and now owned by J. J. Benenson of New York and Maine.
Harold S. Parsons:	Owned a 46 foot 1927 William Hand motorsailer, PENZANCE. A long-time customer, whose family owned much real estate in Brooklyn; he collected rents in person and always carried a gun. The yacht is now owned by Dr. George Scott and was restored in Bayville.
Dr. Cortez Enloe:	His 49 foot powerful 1947 Huckins, named DEVIL'S BELT, looked like a PT boat when underway in the Bay
Fred Voges:	The dashing, silver-haired Errol Flynn type. His immaculate 48 foot FairForm Flyer Huckins, AVOCETTE III, was his pride and joy for 50 years. He purchased this yacht at the 1931 New York Boat Show, and even raced it alongside a cruise ship from Sandy Hook to its New York berth. Sold in 1981, it was later partially damaged by fire; saved by the late Bob Tiedeman of Newport, RI, it then was completely restored by the late Jerry Bass of Bay Head, New Jersey, and is now owned by Earl MacMillen and stored in Newport.

George Hinman	The highly respected, legendary man of yachting; his name and deeds will live on for all of his accomplishments in this field. He owned various boats over the years, but his pale green, 38 foot Concordia, SAGOLA, was wintered in the Marshall boatyard for many years.
Capt. Edward Harrington:	The Jonathan Winters look-alike, Eastern Airlines pilot and member of the Early Flyers Club, used to tell hair-raising flight stories. He has been known to buzz over your boat when you are tucked away in some gunk-hole while he is out test flying. His schooner, the THIRSTY MAJOR, a 45 foot Alden design, was with him for 30 years; now sold and undergoing restoration.
Peter Pannell:	The very British, retired Naval officer who commanded convoy ships during World War II. He always wore high, polished boots and would strut up and down the decks of his very British 38 foot sloop, LARUS, while swinging his crop. Peter Pannell owned LARUS for 45 years. After Peter died, his yacht was sold. He is the father of John Pannell, owner and restorer of the 74 foot APHRODITE.
Charles S. Payson:	Payson owned the 69 foot commuter, SAGA, and the 50 foot WARRIOR powerboat. The Marshall yard maintained WARRIOR.

Charles W. Wittholz:	A noted naval architect, he had his 23 foot sloop, ALBACORE II in the yard for many years during the 1940s.
Leroy Grumman:	A down-to-earth man, who enjoyed working on his own boat, the 48 foot white Chris Craft, SLIPSTREAM.
Phillip Isles:	He and his beautiful Powers model wife were a delightful, stunning couple, owning an equally beautiful 40 foot white Chris Craft, SANDRA VII.
Charles F. Chapman:	Past Editor of Motor Boating and author of *Chapman's Guide to Seamanship and Pilot Handling*, among others. Owned a 22 foot early fiberglass powerboat, CHALMAR. The Chapman Trophy has been an award for junior sailors since 1960.
Fred H. Walsh:	President and Chairman of Cunningham & Walsh, Inc., one of the top advertising agencies in New York in the 1960s. Owned a 50 foot black Schooner, ESCAPE, and later commissioned A & R Marshall, Inc. to build a 50 foot motorsailer, a Neidwedki design. This was the largest boat built at the yard. Fred married Dorothy, Monte and Ray's sister.
Isidor Werbel:	A publisher, he owned a Bristol 55 foot Sparkman & Stephens dashing PORPOISE, which had a flying bridge and was painted a Britannia blue.

Guy LaMotta: Local modern-day developer and owner of Manhasset Bay Marina. Now a retired speedboat racer, he inaugurated the return of the Gold Cup speedboat races that took place on the Bay starting in 1925. He owns a 53 foot, 1969 all-wood Huckins which he had restored, named DRY MARTINI. He also restored an MBO (Manhasset Bay One Design) and has it on display at his marina and restaurant on Manhasset Isle.

Bill Leiber and Jack Kraemer   When these two were young they restored a 1928, 33 foot Gar Wood speedboat, the DAVY JONES (20K) after she was partially destroyed in the 1938 hurricane. She was originally built for Caleb Bragg and later raced by Keenan Wynn, son of Ed Wynn. They went on to win many races and established new speed records in the 1940s and 50s. She was sold in the 60s and was later restored again by the Turcotte Brothers, and won "Antique Boat of the Year" at Clayton, NY in 1989.

CHRONOLOGICAL DATA

403 and 405 Main Street, Port Washington, Long Island, New York:

1906 Property originally owned by Joseph Dondera. Two Buildings; one was the Bayview Hotel, the other a small waterfront pavilion.

1918-1928 Before the move to 403 Main Street, Albert and Raymond Marshall conducted an automotive and supply business at 326 Main Street.

1928 William Eaton sold property to Albert and Raymond Marshall. Lot size was 50' frontage by 150' deep. A & R Marshall, Inc. opened for business September, 1928.

1929 Docks enlarged and crane purchased.

1930 Depression began.

1935 Monte joined the business and built a large workboat.

1935-1938   Two-part boat storage sheds built: (Lot #4, Sec. 5, BL-C), the shed where railway is; (Sawyer & Dolfinger, Manhasset) (Lot #3, Sec. 5, BL-C), the shed fronting Main St.

1938   Machine shop renovated/enlarged.

1947-1948   New brick-façade store building constructed at 403 Main Street.

1955-1956   New brick-façade boat storage shed built at 405 Main Street.

1955-1964   Rented boat storage shed to Philip and Ruth Hunter for summer theater, known as "Towndock Theater," which ran for nine years.

1950s   Purchased Olaf's Bar & Grill across the street (404 Main Street) later known as the "Green Door."

405 Main Street

1964-1975   Leased boatyard facilities to McMichael Yacht Services (September 22, 1964), where they conducted a brokerage business.

1975-1990   Sold to Seth Morrison and Elliott Sims, who conducted a yacht brokerage business known as "FLAGSHIP."

1990   Morrison and Sims sold both parcels of Property to Malcolm Tillum. Plans were to enlarge marina, put in shops. Known as Coastline Yacht Sales, Ltd.

<u>403 Main Street</u>

1968   Sold hardware store business to Kenneth Merkel. The store was then divided into two sections. The left side was operated by Mrs. Merkel as a gift department called Davy Jones' Locker. The machine shop was converted into a tropical fashion boutique. The Merkels operated the business for a number of years until he tired of it, and then rented/leased to a religious organization and a stock brokerage business.

1990   This property was also sold to Malcolm Tillum. As of 1991, the right side of 403 Main Street was the offices of the publication *Long Island Power & Sail* published by Melvin Berger of Port Washington, and the other side was vacant. Later sold to John Thomson, and now divided between Thomson and Brewer Yachts.

LONGTIME EMPLOYEES

NAME	POSITION	YEARS
SANDY (Alexander Alexander)	Nightwatchman	40
JIM PHILIPS	Top Mechanic	40
HARRY AARSHEIM	Top Carpenter	40
BERT COCHRAN	Workman	35
SCOTTY	Workman	30
PAT PATERSON	Store Manager	30
AL CARBONELL	Store Salesman	25

BOOKKEEPERS

DOROTHY MARSHALL WALSH
EDITH TOWNSHEND MARSHALL
EDNA VERMILYEA MARSHALL
PEGGY KELLOGG
BEULAH HULTZ DeMEO
JOAN NINESLING LAWRENCE
EVELYN NEILSEN

Printed in the United States
By Bookmasters